Rainbow

Look for the other books on weather by

Marion Dane Bauer
Rain • Wind • Clouds
Snow • Sun

SIMON SPOTLIGHT

An imprint of Simon & Schuster Children's Publishing Division

1230 Avenue of the Americas, New York, New York 10020

This Simon Spotlight edition May 2016

Text copyright © 2016 by Marion Dane Bauer

Illustrations copyright © 2016 by John Wallace

For information about special discounts for bulk purchases, please contact Simon & Schuster Special

Sales at 1-866-506-1949 or business@simonandschuster.com.

Manufactured in the United States of America 0416 LAK

2 4 6 8 10 9 7 5 3 1

Library of Congress Cataloging-in-Publication Data

Names: Bauer, Marion Dane, author. | Wallace, John, 1966–illustrator.

Title: Rainbow / by Marion Dane Bauer ; illustrated by John Wallace.

Description: First Simon Spotlight hardcover/paperback edition. | New York :

Simon Spotlight, 2016.

Identifiers: LCCN 2015046081| ISBN 9781481463379 (hardcover) |

ISBN 9781481463362 (pbk.)

Subjects: LCSH: Rainbows—Juvenile literature.

Classification: LCC QC976.R2 B38 2016 | DDC 551.56/7—dc23

LC record available at http://lccn.loc.gov/201504608

ISBN 9781481463386 (eBook)

Rainbow

written by Marion Dane Bauer

illustrated by John Wallace

Ready-to-Read

Simon Spotlight
New York   London   Toronto   Sydney   New Delhi

Have you ever seen
a surprise in the sky
on a rainy day?

This is what
can happen.
First a few raindrops fall . . .
plink, plop, plunk.

Then more follow . . .

rat-a-tat-tat.

Millions of raindrops
fill the air.

But then
while the rain is still falling,
the sun peeks out
from behind a cloud.

It shines through
all that rain.
And surprise!

A rainbow arcs
across the sky.

Red,
orange,
yellow,
green,
blue,
indigo,
violet.

How did that rainbow
come to be?

White sunlight
passing through millions
of raindrops
bounces and bends.

The light separates
into different colors.

When you are very lucky
the sunlight bounces twice.
Then you see two rainbows.

Sometimes a rainbow
is upside down.

This is called a sun smile.

21

If the angle of the sun
is just right, you can even see
a rainbow in a fountain

or a waterfall.

Have you heard
the story of the
pot of gold at the end
of every rainbow?

It is a nice story,
but it is not true.
A rainbow does not end.

A rainbow is really a full circle.
We cannot see the circle
from the ground because
the Earth gets in the way.

If you move,
the rainbow will move too.

No two people
see the same rainbow.
What you see depends on where
you are standing.

So next time the sun comes out
while it is still raining,
look up in the sky
and enjoy your very own
rainbow.

And if you stand
with your back
to the sun, the rainbow
will light up the sky.
Your rainbow.

Facts about rainbows:

- If you are facing the sun, you cannot see a rainbow. To see one, your back must be to the sun.

- A ring around the moon—a moondog—is created when moonlight reflects off ice crystals in the air.

- You cannot see all the colors in a rainbow. A rainbow is actually made up of more than a million colors. The human eye cannot see many of those colors.

- Rainbows are usually seen in the morning or evening when the sun is rising or setting. Sunlight needs to strike the raindrops at an angle of 42 degrees to create a rainbow.

- You can create your own rainbow. Stand with your back to the sun and spray a mist of water from a hose. Adjust the angle until you see the rainbow.